Amen

THE STORY OF THE BIBLE
from Eden to Eternity

KRISTIN SCHMUCKER

www.thedailygraceco.com

STUDY CONTRIBUTORS

....

Illustrator:
KATIE LINSTRUM

Editor:
JANA WHITE

Before the world began,
God existed.

God has always been and He always
will be. God has no beginning
and no end.

God is a trinity.

That means that there are three
persons in one God.

The trinity lived in perfect community.
And even before the world began,
God made a plan to redeem
a people for Himself.

God created the world with
the power of His word.

He made the sun, the moon,
the earth,

the plants, the animals, and
everything else that we see.

God made everything, and
it is through His power that
all things exist.

Then God made man and woman.

He made them each unique and He made them to complement each other perfectly. Their names were Adam and Eve.

God gave them some big jobs. They were to take care of the garden, rule the animals, and create a family. The garden was a wonderful place. And best of all, God dwelt with Adam and Eve in this beautiful garden.

But then one day, something bad happened. God had told Adam and Eve not to eat from one tree, and they disobeyed His command.

Though God was holy and good, Adam and Eve believed the lie of the sneaky snake and ate the forbidden fruit.

This was the very first sin and the saddest day there ever was. It was sad because Adam and Eve had disobeyed their good God. And it was sad because sin always has consequences and it separates people from God.

But God made a really big promise
to Adam and Eve that day.

He promised that He would send a rescuer to
save His people from their sins. He promised
that someone would come who would crush
the head of that sneaky snake.

Someday He would come,
but not yet.

Eventually, there was a man named Abraham.

God made a big promise to Abraham. He promised
Abraham that he would have a very big family and live
in a special land, and best of all, He promised that the
rescuer would come from his family.

The only problem was that Abraham was very old,
and he didn't have any children.

God always keeps His promises, and when
Abraham was 100 years old (that is really old),
God gave him and his wife Sarah a son named Isaac.
But Isaac wasn't the rescuer.

Someday the rescuer would come,
but not yet.

Abraham's family grew and grew just as God had promised. Abraham had Isaac, and Isaac had Jacob, and Jacob had children, and his children had children, and his children's children had children. Soon there were millions of people in the family of Abraham.

One time, all of these people lived in a country called Egypt.
They were slaves there, but God was still watching out for them.
God sent a man named Moses to deliver the people. They even
walked right through the middle of the Red Sea on dry land.
Moses pointed toward the day when the rescuer would come.

Someday He would come,
but not yet.

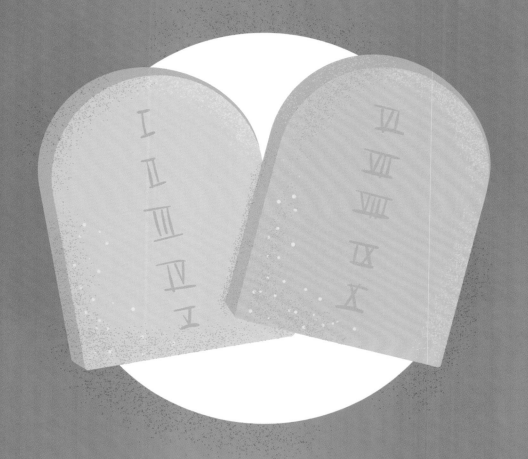

God gave His people the law to teach them how live,
but they just could not obey.

He sent them prophets, and priests, and kings to teach them
the truth, but they liked doing things their own way.
They were still sinning just like Adam and Eve in the garden.
They really needed a rescuer.

Someday He would come, but not yet.

Once there was a king named David.

He loved to worship God. God promised Him that one
day the rescuer would come and be the forever king.
He would sit on the throne forever and ever.
David was a good king, but he still sinned.
David reminds us that we need the forever king.

Someday He would come,
but not yet.

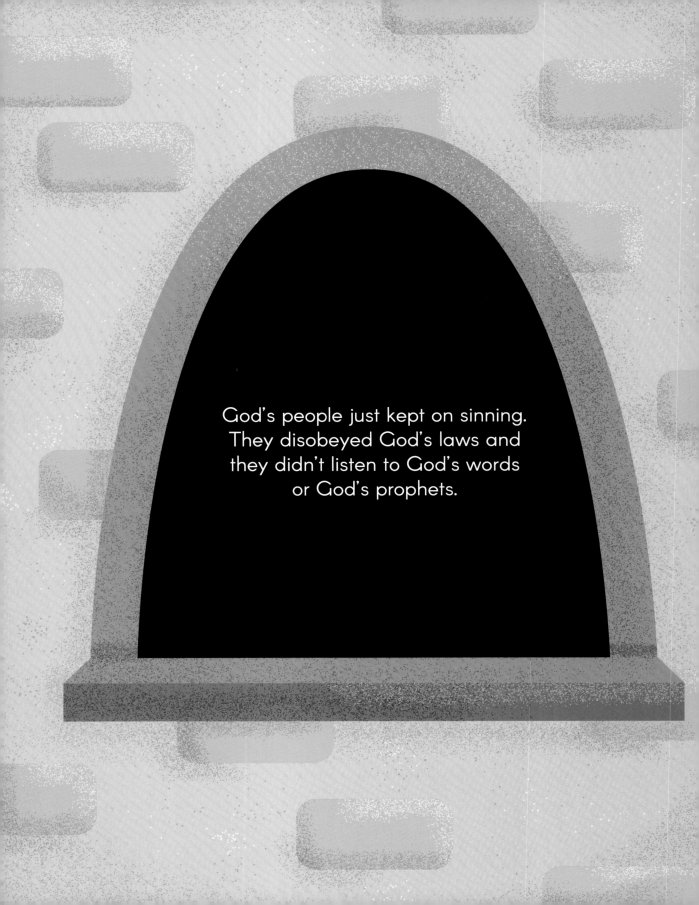

God's people just kept on sinning.
They disobeyed God's laws and
they didn't listen to God's words
or God's prophets.

Then one day God got really quiet.

He didn't send any messages to his people for hundreds of years. Now what was going to happen? Would God still send the rescuer? It seemed like God was silent, but He was working out His perfect plan. God always keeps His promises, and

someday the rescuer would come, but not yet.

Then it happened. After years of silence,
God sent the rescuer. He was born as a tiny baby
in a little town named Bethlehem.

His name was Jesus, and He would save
His people from their sins.

Jesus is totally God and totally man.

God Himself, the second person of the Trinity,
had come down to be the rescuer.

Jesus taught many people about the kingdom of God.
Jesus also did miracles that showed people
that He was God.

Jesus never sinned...not even one time. He lived
the perfect life that we could never live on our own,

and then one day, on a cross, He died the kind of death
that we deserved because of our sin.

On the cross, Jesus died to save sinners.

Jesus' friends were so sad when He died.
How could He be their rescuer if He died?

But three days later, Jesus rose again!

Jesus died because
He is the rescuer.

He died to pay the price of the
sins of His people. Jesus' death
on the cross crushed the head
of that sneaky snake.

The cross reminds us of God's love
and grace for His people.

And the resurrection reminds us
of His power over everything.

God loves
you and
me!

After Jesus rose again, He taught His friends more about what it means to be a disciple and a follower of Jesus.

Then He went back to Heaven.

He gave his people a job to do on earth.
All the followers of Jesus were commanded to bring
glory to God and to share God's message of salvation
with everyone in the whole world!

This might be the end of
the book, but it is not the
end of the story!

Jesus is coming back again.
He is going to make everything new
someday and take away sin and
all of its consequences.

Someday there will be a new heaven
and a new earth, and life for God's
people will be even better than it was
at the very beginning of the story.
Someday we will worship God forever!

Someday Jesus is
coming again!

Thank You

for studying God's
Word with us!